The 5th Wave

The 5th Wave

BYTE-ing Humor by
RICHTENNANT

Andrews and McMeel
A Universal Press Syndicate Company
Kansas City

ISBN: 0-8362-1890-6
Library of Congress Catalog Card Number: 92-70019

First Printing, February 1992
Second Printing, May 1992

To Markin

"I don't think our newest network configuration is going to work. All of our transmissions from Ohio seem to be coming in over my electric pencil sharpener."

"I thought he was a vacuum cleaner salesman. He came in, sprinkled dirt on the carpet, and then tried to sell me a software program that would show me how to clean it up."

"All right, steady everyone. Margo, go over to Tom's PC and press 'ESCAPE' . . . very carefully."

"No, the solution to our system being down is *not* for us to work on our knees."

"Oh, sure, it's nice working at home. Except my boss drives by every morning and blasts his horn to make sure I'm awake."

"I guess there's a 'Users Group' for just about everyone these days."

" . . . And for the high-tech man in your life, we have this lovely PC-on-a-rope."

"A portable computer? You'd better talk to old Bob over there. He's owned a portable longer than anyone here."

"Hold on. That's not a program error, it's just a booger on the screen."

"It's not that it doesn't work as a computer; it just works better as a paperweight."

"You idiot! You drag a mainframe computer onto a life raft and you forget to bring a surge protector?!"

"Gather around, kids. Your mother's windowing!"

"Not only did we get you an apple with a mouse like you asked, we also got you a banana with a lizard."

"I always back up everything."

"There you are, sir. One MacPaint, a MacWrite, a MacAccountant, two MacSlots, a MacPhone, and a MacDraw. Would you like fries with that?"

"Yeah, my people are still getting headaches — dang these VDT screens!"

"What do you mean it sort of is and isn't compatible?"

"Gary and some of his friends wanted to bob for Apples this year. I guess it can't hurt as long as they're not plugged in."

"Right now I'm keeping a low profile. Last night I cranked it all up and blew out three blocks of streetlights."

"Apparently most studies indicate that what people really want isn't more power or increased applications, but just really neat tail fins."

Poet e.e. cummings makes his last service call.

"I *saaiid* what company do you represent?"

"Well, right off, the response time seems a bit slow."

"I said I wanted a new monitor for my birthday!
Monitor! Monitor!"

"The image is getting clearer now.... I can almost see
it.... Yes! There it is—the glitch is in a faulty cable at
your office in Denver."

In a display of perverse brilliance, Carl the Repairman mistakes a room humidifier for a mid-range computer, but manages to tie it into the network anyway.

AFTER THE INITIAL MERGER OF TWO COMPANIES COMES THE DELICATE PROCESS OF SELECTING A DOMINANT SOFTWARE SYSTEM.

SOMEONE SAY "GO".

"This security program will respond to three things: an incorrect access code, an inappropriate file request, or sometimes a crazy hunch that maybe you're just another slime-ball with misappropriation of secured data on his mind."

"Well, Mr. Bond, I guess this is farewell. Lower . . . the . . . laser . . . printer!"

"Do you want me to call the company and have them send another review copy of their database software system, or do you know what you're going to write?"

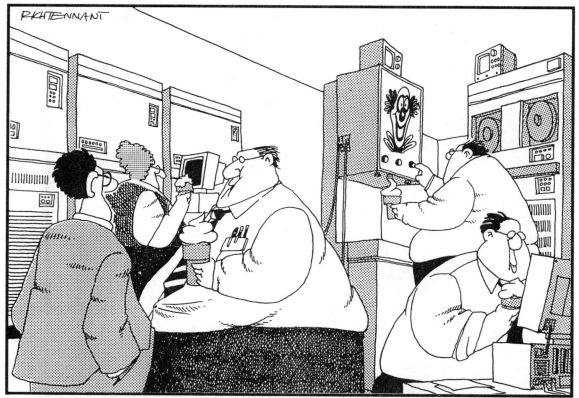

"We're using a four-tiered system — PC to mini to Mr. Smoothy to mainframe."

After spending nine days with twelve different vendors and reading twenty-six brochures, Dave had an acute attack of Toxic Option Syndrome.

"I just don't think this new sales kid is gonna work out."

"Who's got the computer with the slow response time?"

"How should I know why they took it off the list?
Maybe there just weren't enough members to support
an Airedales for Elvis Bulletin Board."

"It started out as a kit, and while I was waiting for parts,
they merged with a vacuum cleaner company."

"C'mon, Brickman, you know as well as I do that 'nose-scanning' is our best defense against unauthorized access to personal files."

"I'm afraid I don't understand all the reports of our upgrade having a delayed release date, unless . . . wait a minute—how many people here *didn't* know I was speaking in dog-months?"

"Let me guess—no surge protectors . . . right?"

"No, no! You high-five them on the hand! The hand! Not the face!"

"Oh, sure, $1.8 million seems like a lot right now, but what about Randy? What about his future? Think what a computer like this will do for his S.A.T. scores someday."

"A story about a software company that ships bug-free programs on time, with toll-free support and free upgrades? Naaah — too weird."

"Well, Personal Information Management Software helps show you the connection between seemingly disparate items, like, oh, say, that tie you're wearing, and this bowl of goat vomit."

"He said the only heavy metal he was into was mainframes."

Bob, the laser printer salesman, finds an idle moment that costs him most of his facial hair.

"We offer a creative MIS environment working with state-of-the-art equipment, a comprehensive benefits package, generous stock options, and, if you're feeling funky and want to rap, we can do that, too."

"I don't get it. We've made it smaller, faster, and less expensive, and it still doesn't sell! Jeez, Bobby, don't lean on the mouse like that."

"If you think we've had tough service calls up to now,
wait'll you meet this guy."

"A consultant told us that polyester can cause shorts
in the system. So we're trying an all-leather and
Spandex data entry department."

"We test for compatibility, performance, service, and formatting. If it fails these, then it's tested for the distance it can be sailed across the parking lot and onto the expressway."

"Oops— here's the problem. Something's causing shorts in the mainframe."

30 Years ago today...

Bill and Irwin Fuzzo, two plumbers from Eugene, Oregon developed the first hydro-pneumatic PC. It could be connected to an average garden hose, and response time was increased by "...squeezing the hose a little bit." Software was to be developed by a local manufacturer of squirt guns... 30 Years Ago Today!

On a bet, Howie Lendelman, the office tinkerer, tries linking his T.I. calculator into the workgroup's Deskpro 386/25 Network File Server.

PROVING THAT BIGGER ISN'T ALWAYS BEST, A CONTRACT TO BUILD A COMPUTERIZED SONAR TRACKING SYSTEM FOR THE U.S. NAVY IS AWARDED TO TROOP 708 OF THE BAYONNE, NEW JERSEY EAGLE SCOUTS.

So poorly documented is the software that Roy is Beta testing, that he fails to notice that the game rules to Twister have accidentally been included.

"'Morning, Mr. Drexel. I heard you say your computers all had bugs. Well, I figure they're crawling in through those slots they have, so I jammed a couple of roach-disks in each one. Let me know if you have any more problems."

"Better call MIS and tell them one of our networks has gone bad."

49

"The manufacturer of a data encryption program that scrambles messages into a brainless morass of indecipherable code, has just filed a 'look and feel' copyright suit against our word processing program."

" ... And tell the Chief Information Officer that system integration shouldn't be a problem with this buyout. Their computers all seem to be pretty much the same color as ours."

"We figure the equipment must have scared her away. A few days after setting up, little Snowball just disappeared."

"The phone company blames the manufacturer, who says it's the software company's fault, who blames it on our moon being in Venus with Scorpio rising."

LARRY, THE BALLOON MAN, EMPLOYS A CAD/CAM SOFTWARE PACKAGE INTO HIS BALLOON ANIMAL ACT.

LARRY the BALLOON MAN

"Excuse me, ma'am — Royal Canadian Mounted Programmers — someone here report a missing file?"

"Hello, Smart-Home Maintenance? Can you send someone out—our den is acting really stupid."

"All right, now we need someone to play the part of the geek."

"Naaah — he's not that smart. He won't back up his hard disk, consistently forgets to name his files, and drools all over the keyboard."

"I wish someone would explain to Professor Jones that you don't need a whip and a leather jacket to find a lost file."

"It's amazing how much more some people can get out of a PC than others."

"The LCD display was good, plasma displays were a little better, but we think the liquid lava display that Jerry's developed is gonna rock the industry."

"Look, I have no problem running Mickey-micros and Pluto-PCs through a Tinkerbell bus, but we're never going to have a Huey-Dewey-Louie-LAN on a Minnie-mini without seriously upgrading all of our Goofy software."

"Call me crazy, but I've got a hunch this virus was generated internally."

"These kidnappers are clever, lieutenant. Look at this ransom note, the way they got the text to wrap around the victim's photograph. And the fonts! They must be creating their own — must be over thirty-five typefaces here. . . ."

"Oh, those? They're seat-cushion-mouses; bounce once to access a file, twice to file away—
keeps the hands free and helps firm the buttocks."

RAYMOND BUTZLE BREAKS THE BATTERY BARRIER IN LAP-TOPS BY ADAPTING HIS "POTATO CLOCK" TO A COMPUTER, THUS CREATING THE FIRST 12 MIPS, 8 MBYTE, 6 SPUD SYSTEM.

"Yo, Mr. Jackson, found the problem! Seems a glove was jammin' up the printer!"

"It's a software program that more fully reflects an actual office environment. It multi-tasks with other users, integrates shared data, and then uses that information to network vicious rumors through an inter-office link-up."

Tom's company occasionally conducted spot checks to make sure the employees weren't sneaking their Macintoshes into the office.

"It's about a group of young, inexperienced German programmers all cramped together inside this hot, tiny computer room fighting the virus of their lives during the early years of network communications."

66

"It was clashing with the southwestern motif."

IN THE AFTERMATH OF ANOTHER FAILED BID TO CAPTURE THE HOME COMPUTER MARKET, KLIEN'S DEPARTMENT STORE ATTEMPTS TO UNLOAD ITS INVENTORY OF CHIA-PET PC's.

Y'KNOW, I DON'T MIND LIVING IN A COMPUTERIZED 'SMART HOUSE,' BUT I DO MIND BEING CALLED AN IDIOT BY THE TOASTER.

In the history of the personal computer, Mel and Frank's "Lube 'n Tune" represented the first true garage start-up.
RICHTENNANT
Whoa, Mel,-printer's low on ink.
DELCO
DELCO

"Gentlemen, I say rather than fix the 'bugs,' we change the documentation and call them 'features.'"

YEAH, BUT YOU SHOULD SEE HOW NICELY IT CENTERED EVERYTHING.

"No, they're not really a gang, just a particularly aggressive LAN."

"Oddly enough, it does improve PC performance. But you've got to make sure your nitro to ethyl-methylene mixture is just right, or you'll crash the disk drive and crap out the valves."

"Well, systems integration isn't perfect. Some departments *still* seem to get more information than others."

"Oh, yeah, and try not to enter the wrong password."

"Hey, I never saw a slow response time fixed with a paperweight before."

" . . . And talk about memory! This baby's got so much memory, it comes with extra documentation, a hard disk, and a sense of guilt! I mean *I'm* talkin' memory.'"

WHILE SEEKING HER PC-BASED RECIPE INDEX, LORRETTA INADVERTENTLY LOADS A CAD/CAM PROGRAM. INSTEAD OF MAKING CHERRIES JUBILEE, SHE BUILDS A SUBOCEANIC DIVING PROBE.

"Here on Altair-14, we've implemented anything-to-anything integration."

"And just what the heck part of the network *did* you say you're from?"

"We run the company a lot like a college. We stay up late cramming to finish software products, encourage study groups with multi-user networks, and on Fridays we all gather in the cafeteria, dance, drink, and throw up on our shoes."

"Unfortunately, the system's not very fault-tolerant."

"Yeah, I've finished reviewing the monitor, keyboard, CPU, and printer, and I'm just finishing up my review of the mouse right now."

"I told him we were looking for software that would give us greater productivity, so he sold me a spreadsheet that came with these signs."

IN A STROKE OF SELF-RELIANCE, RAY EXTENDS THE POWER ON HIS LAPTOP BY TAPPING INTO THE BATTERY ON HIS SLEEPING NEIGHBOR'S HEARING AID.

"Oh, Scarecrow—I don't think you'll need your laptop in the Emerald City anyway."

"For additional software support, dial '9,' 'pound,' the extension number divided by your account number, hit 'star,' your dog, blow into the receiver twice, punch in your hat size, punch out your landlord . . ."

"There! There! I tell you if just moved again!"

"Yeah, I started the company right after I graduated from college. How'd you guess?"

"No, you're in the castle computer room. That's the 'Wizard of Nerd.' You want 'Oz'—two doors down on your right."

"Frankly, I'm not sure this is the way to enhance our color graphics."

"It says here if I subscribe to this magazine, they'll send me a free desktop calculator. *Desktop* calculator?!! Whooaa—where have *I* been?!!"

"It's no use, Captain. The only way we'll crack this case is to get into Prof. Tamara's personal computer file, but no one knows the password. Kilroy's got a hunch it starts with an 's,' but, heck, that could be anything."

"Our new program application has been on the market for over six months, and not a single copyright infringement lawsuit has been brought against us. I'm worried."

93

"I'm gonna have a little trouble with this 'full moon' icon on our graphical user's interface."

"Wow! I didn't even think they *made* a 2000-dot-per-inch font!"

"Wait a minute! The monster seems confused, disoriented. I think he's gonna pass out! Get the nets ready!!"

"Yeah, I used to work on refrigerators, washing machines, stuff like that—how'd you guess?"

Under pressure to increase productivity, the systems manager at Mondo Corp. reads that computer chips run faster at colder temperatures. . . .

"Why don't you take that outside, Humpty, and play with it on the wall?"

"I'm paying $28,000 a year to an Ivy League university so that you can become an expert in artificial intelligence?"

MY GOD! IT'S WORKING! I'M GETTING ITALICS!

"The artist was also a programmer and evidently produced several variations on this theme."

"Let's see — the National Guard has a C-130 heading
in that direction, or you could hitch a ride with the
'Sky-Eye' traffic copter; have you ever flown with
a crop duster before, Mr. Peterson?"

"Okay, let's see. If we can all remain calm and stop
acting crazy, I'm sure I'll eventually remember what
name I filed the antidote under."